Also by C. K. Williams

Lies   (1969)
I Am the Bitter Name   (1971)
With Ignorance   (1977)
Sophocles' Women of Trachis (with Gregory Dickerson)   (1978)
The Lark. The Thrush. The Starling.: Poems from Issa   (1983)
Tar   (1983)
Flesh and Blood   (1987)
Poems 1963–1983   (1989)
The Bacchae of Euripides   (1990)

A Dream of Mind

A DREAM OF MIND

Poems

C. K. WILLIAMS

Farrar, Straus and Giroux

New York

Library of Congress Cataloging-in-Publication Data
Williams, C. K. (Charles Kenneth).
  A dream of mind : poems / C. K. Williams. — 1st ed.
  I. Title.
  PS3573.I4483D74 1992   811'.54—dc20   92-2951 CIP

Some of these poems have appeared in the following
publications: "When" and "The Mirror" in *The New
Yorker.* "Helen" in *The American Poetry Review* and *The
Irish Review.* A signed, limited edition was also published
in November 1991 by Orchises Press of Alexandria,
Virginia. "Allies: According to Herodotus," "Chapter
Eleven," "Harm," "The Cautionary," "Pillow Talk," and
"Ethics" in *The Times Literary Supplement.* From the
sequence "A Dream of Mind," "History" first appeared in
Tikkun, "Room" and "The Knot" in *Antaeus,* and "The
Gap" in *The Threepenny Review.* "She, Though" first
appeared in *TriQuarterly,* a publication of Northwestern
University. "Signs" in *The Madison Review,* in a different
version, under the title "Soldiers." "Scar" and, from "A
Dream of Mind," "The Crime," "To Listen," and "The
Covenant" in *The Kenyon Review."* "Politics" and "The
Idyll" in *Phoebe*

for
Tex and Barbara
and
Lynn and Bob

Contents

4
A Dream of Mind

5

1

When

As soon as the old man knew he was actually dying, even before anyone
    else would admit it,
he wanted out of the business, out of the miserable game, and he told
    whoever would listen,
whenever they'd listen, wife, family, friends, that he'd do it himself but
    how could he,
without someone to help, unable to walk as he was, get out of bed or
    up from the toilet himself?

At first he'd almost been funny: "Somebody comes, somebody goes,"
    he'd said on the birth of a niece,
and one day at lunch, "Please pass the cream cheese," then, deadpan,
    "That's all I'll miss."
But now he's obsessed: "Why won't you help me?" he says to his children,
    ten times a day,
a hundred and ten, but what if such meddling's wrong, and aren't these
    last days anyway precious?

Still, he was wearing them down: "This is no fun," he said to a son
    helping him hobble downstairs,
and the son, knowing full well what he meant, dreading to hear what
    he meant, had to ask "What?"
so the old man, the biopsy incision still lumping the stubble of hair on
    the side of his skull,
could look in his eyes and say, if not as an accusation then nearly, "Death,
    dying: you know."

By then they knew, too, that sooner or later they'd have to give in, then
    sooner was over,
only later was looming, aphasiac, raving too late, so they held council
    and argued it out,
and though his daughter, holding onto lost hopes, was afraid, they decided
    to help him,

and told the old man, who said, "Finally, at last," and then to his
daughter, "Don't be afraid."

On the day it would happen, the old man would be funny again: wolfing
down handfuls of pills,
"I know this'll upset my stomach," he'd say, but for now he only asks
how it will happen.
"You'll just sleep," he's told, and "That's great" is his answer: "I haven't
slept for weeks."
Then "Great" again, then, serious, dry-eyed, to his weeping family: "Just
don't tell me when."

The Vessel

I'm trying to pray; one of the voices of my mind says, "God, please help
    me do this,"
but another voice intervenes: "How conceive God's interest would be to
    help you believe?"

Is this prayer? Might this exercise be a sign, however impure, that such
    an act's under way,
that I'd allowed myself, or that God had allowed me, to surrender to this
    need in myself?

What makes me think, though, that the region of my soul in which all
    this activity's occurring
is a site which God might consider an engaging or even an acceptable
    spiritual location?

I thought I'd kept the lack of a sacred place in myself from myself,
    therefore from God.
Is *this* prayer, recognizing that my isolation from myself is a secret I no
    longer can keep?

Might prayer be an awareness that even our most belittling secrets are
    absurd before God?
Might God's mercy be letting us think we haven't betrayed those secrets
    to Him until now?

If I believe that there exists a thing I can call God's mercy, might I be
    praying at last?
If I were, what would it mean: that my sad loneliness for God might be
    nearing its end?

I imagine that were I in a real relation with God instead of just being
    lonely for Him,
the way I'd apprehend Him would have nothing to do with secrets I'd
    kept, from Him or myself.

I'd empty like a cup: that would be prayer, to empty, then fill with a substance other than myself.

Empty myself of what, though? And what would God deign fill me with except my own prayer?

Is this prayer now, believing that my offering to God would be what He'd offered me?

I'm trying to pray, but I know that whatever I'm doing I'm not: why aren't I, when will I?

Allies: According to Herodotus

"Just how much are you worth?" Xerxes asks Pythius, reputedly the richest
    man in Lydia,
at the entertainment Pythius was holding in his palace for Xerxes and
    his chiefs of staff.
"Exactly three million nine hundred and ninety-three thousand golden
    darics," Pythius answers,
"and all of it is yours, my humble contribution towards your glorious
    war against the Greeks."

Xerxes is pleased: since he's left Persia with his troops, only Pythius along
    their route
has offered hospitality without being compelled to; all this might indicate
    a welcome drift.
"Consider yourself my personal friend," he says to Pythius: "Keep your
    fortune, you've earned it,
and furthermore I'm awarding you another seven thousand darics of my
    own to round it off."

Later, as Xerxes is preparing to go on, an eclipse is sighted, which ir-
    rationally alarms Pythius,
but also encourages him to ask Xerxes for a favor. "Anything you want
    just ask," says Xerxes.
"I have five sons," Pythius replies, "and all of them are leaving to take
    part in your campaign.
I'm getting on: let me keep my eldest here, to help take care of me and
    see to my estates."

Xerxes is incensed. "You ungrateful scum," he snarls, "you have the gall
    to talk about your son,
when I myself, Xerxes himself, is going off to fight with all my sons and
    friends and relatives?
It would have pleased my ears if you'd offered me your *wife*, and thrown
    in your old carcass.

You saved yourself by your generosity the other night, but now you'll
    know a real king's rage."

Some ancients doubt Herodotus, but not in this; Xerxes, after all, angry
    at the Hellespont,
had it lashed and branded; we can trust therefore that near the moment
    when history begins,
Xerxes commanded that the beloved elder son of Pythius be brought to
    him and cut in half,
and that the halves be placed along the roadside for his army to march
    out towards Greece between.

Harm

With his shopping cart, his bags of booty and his wine, I'd always found
    him inoffensive.
Every neighborhood has one or two these days; ours never rants at you
    at least or begs.

He just forages the trash all day, drinks and sings and shadowboxes, then
    at nightfall
finds a doorway to make camp, set out his battered little radio and slab
    of rotting foam.

The other day, though, as I was going by, he stepped abruptly out between
    parked cars,
undid his pants, and, not even bothering to squat, sputtered out a noxious,
    almost liquid stream.

There was that, and that his bony shanks and buttocks were already stained
    beyond redemption,
that his scarlet testicles were blown up bigger than a bull's with some
    sorrowful disease,

and that a slender adolescent girl from down the block happened by right
    then, and looked,
and looked away, and looked at me, and looked away again, and made
    me want to say to her,

because I imagined what she must have felt, It's not like this, really, it's
    not this,
but she was gone, so I could think, But isn't it like this, isn't this just
    what it is?

The Insult

Even here, in a forest in the foothills of a range of mountains, lucent
     air, the purest dawn,
a continent and years away from where it happened, it comes back to
     me, simmering and stinging,
driving me farther down along the pathway to a hidden brook I hadn't
     realized was there.

The thrust came first, accurate, deft, to the quick, its impetus and rea-
     sonings never grasped.
Then my pain, my sullen, shocked retort, harsh, but with nothing like
     an equivalent rancor.
Then the subsiding: nothing resolved, only let slide; nothing forgiven,
     only put by.

The stream bends here under a bridge, its voice lifts more loudly from
     the rocks of its bed.
The quickly hardening light slants in over the tough, sparse wild grasses
     on the far hill.
Wind rattling the aspens; a hawk so tiny it seems almost a toy hovering
     in a socket of updraft.

Even now, I have no real wish to tell it, I know it so well why have to
     recite it again?
What keeps bringing us back to those fissures so tenaciously holding our
     furious suffering?
Are there deeper wounds in us than we know; might grief itself be com-
     munion and solace?

So many footprints crossing and recrossing the trail through the boulders
     edging the bank;
the swarms of apparently purposeless insects ticking their angular circuits
     over the water.
The song of the water, the mindless air, the hawk beyond sight, the
     inaudible cry of its prey.

Child Psychology

For Loren Crabtree and Barbara Cram

In that stage of psychosexual development called latency, when not that
much, at least supposedly,
is going on—libido sleeps, the engrossing Oedipal adventure is forgotten
for a time—
we were going somewhere and without telling him I took my father's
keys and went outside to wait.
House, car, office keys: how proud I was to be the keeper of that weighty,
consequential mass.
I stood there, tossing it from hand to hand, then, like my father, high
into the air.
And then I missed, and saw it fall, onto the narrow grating of a storm
sewer, and then in.

I gazed, aghast, down into those viscous, unforgiving depths, intestinal,
malignant, menacing.
What happened? Had I dropped the keys on purpose? God no: I well
knew my father's hand.
They'd just fallen, by themselves, that's what I'd say; no, say nothing,
that was even better,
keep still, lips sealed, stoicism, silence—what other mechanism did I
have beside denial?
Which is what I implemented when my father came to question me,
and question me again.
Wholly taken in the burning ardor of my virtue, I was as innocent as
Isaac, and as dumb.

Months pass, the doorbell rings, as always I'm the one to run to answer;
a man is there,
he holds the long-forgotten ring of keys, my father's name, address, and
number legible, intact.
I don't remember what men wore back then to muck about in filth for
us, but it didn't matter;
the second I saw him I knew him—*the return of the repressed . . .* so
soon, though, so very soon.

The shudderings I drove within were deafening; I couldn't bring myself
       to speak, but knew he would,
as I knew what he would say: "Is your father home?" He was, he was:
       how could he not be?

Chapter Eleven

As in a thousand novels but I'll never as long as I live get used to this
    kind of thing,
the guy who works as director of something or other in the business my
    friend owns and who,
I'm not sure why, we're out, my friend and I, for an after-work drink
    with, keeps kidding around,
making nice, stroking us, both of us, but of course mostly my friend,
    saying "Yes, boss, yes, boss,"
which is supposed to be funny but isn't because joke or no joke he's really
    all over my friend,
nodding, fawning, harking hard, and so intense it all is, with such edges
    of rage or despair—
is my friend letting him go? is his job as they say in that world, that hard
    world, on the line?—
that finally even my friend, who must have suspected something like this
    was going to happen
(why bring me then?), gets edgy, there are lapses, we all shift, then my
    friend says something,
"I don't feel great," something, "I have a headache," and, without think-
    ing, I'm sure without thinking,
it happens so quickly, the guy reaches, and, with the back of his hand,
    like a nurse or a mother,
feels my friend's forehead, as though to see if he has a fever, and my
    friend, what else? jerks back,
leaving the hand hung there in mid-air for a moment, almost saluting,
    almost farewelling,
until finally the poor man hauls the hand in, reels it back in, and does
    what with it?
Puts it for a moment lightly on the back of his head, lightly on his collar,
    the table, his drink?
All right, yes, the back of his head, lightly; lightly, his collar, the table,
    his drink.
But what does it matter anyway what the poor man does with his poor
    marooned hand?

Besides, he's fine now, we're all fine, it was all just a blink, the man's folded his hands,
you'd think he was just saying grace or something, and probably nothing happened at all,
you probably just blinked and drifted and imagined it all; if you asked the man how he was,
what would he say, except "What do you mean?" and what would you do but shut up and smile,
this isn't the *Death of a Salesman*, nobody here is going to turn into a Gregor Samsa;
if you were him, wouldn't the last thing you'd want be for someone like me to me-too you?
My friend beckons, the check comes on its little salver and my friend stares down at it hard.
"I'm dead," he says finally. "I'm on such a short leash with the bank, I can't make a dime."

The Loneliness

Not even when my gaze had gone unmet so long, starved so long, it
    went out of my control;
the most casual passing scrutiny would make my eyes, though I'd implore
    them not to,
scurry, slither, dart away to execute again their cowardly, abject ceremony
    of submission.

It was as though my pupils had extruded agonizing wires anyone who
    wanted to could tug.
What I looked at, what let approach me, had virtue only in so much as
    it would let me be,
let me hide further back within myself, let that horrid, helpless, sideways
    cringing stop.

Not even when my voice became so riddled with disuse my only recourse
    seemed to be to cry.
Some pointless pride, though, wouldn't let me: I'd ransack the layers of
    numb, resisting tissue,
but when I'd touch my cheeks they'd still be dry, even that benign release
    had been proscribed.

I'd think there might be something I could tell myself that would be
    equivalent to crying,
an idea or locution that would excavate a route through those impacted
    wells of desolation.
Thought hurt now, though; I couldn't concentrate: the most elementary
    logic lay beyond me.

Not even when, near sleep, it seemed somewhere in my mental boil my
    name was being called.
I'd reach out to hold the voice, then I'd realize that "name" and "call"
    were only symbols,
that some more painful aural stuff was solidifying in the echoing am-
    phitheater of my skull.

No wonder my fascination turned to those as lost as me, the drugged,
    the drunk, the mad.
Like ancient wounds they were, punctured with their solitude and sorrow,
    suppurating, stinking;
I'd recoil from what the soul could come to, but I knew within my soul
    that they were me.

My life, too, eluded me; I, too, learned to shun what of myself I saw in
    those around me.
No face now without its screen of categorical resistance, no glance un-
    tainted by denial.
I was being spoored by my imaginations; I felt guilt, and then remorse,
    as though I'd sinned.

I thought I'd come to know it then, when it began to turn on me, become
    its own exacerbation,
when the most unpremeditated look or smile or gesture, coming from it
    didn't matter who,
roused only rage in me, rejection, fire . . . I was close then, closer, but
    no, not even then.

By then, though, I was near the end; I'd never thought I would, but I
    was looking back,
almost apprehensive for the innocent I'd been, wondering if it all had
    been a romance,
if I might have really sanctioned all that hard annealing, and even then
    I hadn't understood.

When I knew, it was long after I imagined that I'd let it go; when I saw
    it come upon my children;
when I knew that they believed as I'd believed they'd never be sufficient
    to themselves again;
when I realized there was nothing I could do or say to help them: then,
    and only then.

Scar

As though the skin had been stripped and pulled back onto the skull like
    a stocking and soldered
too tightly so that it mottled to yellow and ocher, the pores and follicles
    thumbed out of the clay
by the furious slash of flame that must have leapt on her and by the
    healing that hurt her—

if it is healing that leaves her, age three, in a lassitude lax on her mother's
    broad lap,
bleak, weary, becalmed, what's left of her chin leaned heavily onto what's
    left of her fingers,
those knobs without nails, diminished, blunted, as though someone had
    hammered them thicker;

nares gone, ears gone, most of the dear lips gone so that your gaze is
    taken too deeply, terribly,
into the pool of the mouth as into a genital; the eyelids upper and lower
    wrinkled like linen,
the blood rims of the eyes too graphically vivid; harsh, tearless, porno-
    graphically red—

and you are supposed not to look or look and glance quickly away and
    not look at the mother,
who signs with a stone shoulder and eyes fixed to the child's white-gauze
    surgical cap
that if you do look you are cursed, if you do look you will and you well
    know it be damned.

Lascivious pity, luxurious pity, that glances and looks and looks twice
    and delivers the tear
and hauls out of the blind, locked caves of the breast these silent strangles
    of sobs
that ache but give something like tremulous whispers of sanctity back,
    psalms of gratification.

Lascivious pity, idle, despicable pity, pity of the reflexive half-thought
    holy thought
thinking the mindless threnody of itself once again: I watched, I couldn't
    not watch her,
as she so conscientiously, carefully wouldn't watch me; rapacious, pil-
    laging pity: forgive me.

2

Some of the Forms

of Jealousy

Signs

My friend's wife has a lover; I come to this conclusion—not suspicion,
    mind, conclusion,
not a doubt about it, not a hesitation, although how I get there might
    be hard to track;
a blink a little out of phase, say, with its sentence, perhaps a word or
    two too few;
a certain tenderness of atmosphere, of aura, almost like a pregnancy,
    with less glow, perhaps,
but similar complex inward blushes of accomplishment, achievement,
    pride—during dinner,
as she passes me a dish of something, as I fork a morsel of it off, as our
    glances touch.

My friend's manner, or his guise, is openness, heartiness and healthy
    haleness in all things;
the virtue of conviction, present moment, that sort of thing: it is his
    passion and his ethic,
so I don't know now if he knows or doesn't know, or knows and might
    be hiding it, or doesn't care.
He is hearty, open, present; he is eating dinner in the moment with his
    wife and old dear friend.
The wife, wifely, as she pours my wine and hands it to me looks across
    the glass's rim at me.
Something in the wifely glance tells me now she knows I know, and
    when I shyly look away,
reach across for bread and butter, she looks down at my hand, and up
    again: she is telling me
she doesn't care the least bit if I know or don't know, she might in fact
    wish me to know.

My friend is in the present still, taking sustenance; it's sustaining, good;
    he smiles, good.
Down below, I can just make out the engines of his ship, the stresses,
    creaks, and groans;

everything's in hand; I hear the happy workers at their chugging furnaces
and boilers.
I let my friend's guise now be not my guise but truth; in truth, I'm like
him, dense, convinced,
involved all in the moment, hearty, filled, fulfilled, not just with manner,
but with fact.
I ply my boilers, too; my workers hum: light the deck lamps, let the string
quartet play.

My friend's wife smiles and offers me her profile now; she is telling me
again: but why?
She smiles again, she glows, she plays me like a wind chime; I sit here
clanging to myself.
My friend doesn't seem to see me resonating; he grins, I grin, too, I flee
to him again.
I'm with him in his moment now, I'm in my mouth just as he's in his,
munching, hungrily, heartily.
My safe and sane and hungry mouth hefts the morsels of my sustenance
across its firmament.
The wife smiles yet again, I smile, too, but what I'm saying is if what
she means is so,
I have no wish to know; more, I never did know; more, if by any chance
I might have known,
I've forgotten, absolutely, yes: if it ever did come into my mind it's slipped
my mind.
In truth, I don't remember anything; I eat, I drink, I smile; I hardly even
know I'm there.

The Cautionary

A man who's married an attractive, somewhat younger woman conceives
a painful jealousy of her.
At first he's puzzled as to why he should brood so fretfully on her faith-
fulness or lack of it.
Their lovemaking is fulfilling: he enjoys it, his wife seems to, too, as
much as he does,
or, to his surprise (he's never had this experience before), maybe more
than he does.
When they married, it had seemed a miracle, he'd hardly been able to
believe his great luck:
the ease and grace with which she'd come to him, the frank, good-
humored way she'd touch him.
But now . . . it isn't that she gives too much meaning to sex, or exhibits
insufficient affection,
it's how *involved* in it she gets, so nearly oblivious, in a way he can never
imagine being.
He finds that he's begun to observe their life in bed with what he thinks
is a degree of detachment.
He sees himself, his blemishes, the paunch he can't always hide, then
her, her sheen, her glow.
Why, he asks, would such a desirable woman have committed herself
so entirely to such as him?
And, more to the point: why this much passion, these urgencies and
wants, this blind delight?
By a train of logic he can't trace to its source but which he finds chillingly
irrefutable,
he decides that it's not he himself, as himself, his wife desires, but that
she simply *desires.*
He comes to think he's incidental to this desire, which is general, un-
specific, without object,
almost, in its intensity and heat, without a subject: she herself seems
secondary to it,
as though the real project of her throaty, heaving passion was to melt
her mindlessly away.

Why would such need be limited to him: wouldn't it sweep like a search-
light across all maleness?
He can't help himself, he begins to put to the proof his disturbing but
compelling observations.
When they're out together, it's self-evident to him that every man who
sees her wants her:
all the furtive glances, behind, aside, even into surfaces that hold her
image as she passes.
It dawns on him in a shocking and oddly exciting insight that for so many
to desire her
some *signal* would have to be sent, not an actual gesture perhaps, nothing
so coarse as a beckoning,
but something like an aura, of eagerness, availability, which she'd be
subconsciously emitting.
Hardly noticing, he falls a step behind her, the better to watch her, to
keep track of her.
Then he realizes to his chagrin that his scrutiny might very well be
working on his wife.
In a sadly self-fulfilling prophecy, she might begin to feel vulnerable,
irritated, disconnected;
yes, alone, she must often feel alone, as though he, wretch that he is,
wasn't even there.
This is the last way he'd have thought that his obsession would undo
him, but why not?
A woman among admiring men is already in the broadest sense a potential
object of desire,
but a woman with a sharply heightened awareness of her most elementary
sexual identity,
as his wife by now would have, with this jackal, as he now sees himself,
sniffing behind her:
wouldn't she, even against her best intentions, manifest this in a primitive,
perceptible way,
and wouldn't men have to be aware, however vaguely, that some sexual
event was taking place?
Mightn't the glances she'd inspire reflect this, bringing an intriguing new
sense of herself,
and mightn't this make even more likely that she'd betray him in just
the way that he suspects?

Yes. No. Yes. He knows that he should stop all this: but how can he,
 without going to the end?
The end might be just the thing he's driving them both towards, he can't
 help himself, though,
he'll dissemble his fixations, but if there's to be relief, it will have to wait
 till then.

Baby Talk

Willa Selenfriend likes Paul Peterzell better than she likes me and I am
      dying of it.
"Like" is what we say in eighth grade to mean a person has a secret crush
      on someone else.
I am dying of Willa liking Paul without knowing why she likes him more,
      or what it means.
It doesn't matter, Willa has insinuated cells of doubt in me, I already
      feel them multiplying,
I know already that a single lifetime won't be long enough to extirpate
      their progeny.
Willa likes Paul better than me but one summer day she'll come out to
      the park with me.
Why? Did she pity me? I don't care. We're there, we've walked, now
      we're resting on the grass.
Is this rest, though, to lie here, Willa so close, as lovely as ever, and as
      self-possessed?
I try, too, to calm myself, but the silence is painful; is this because Paul's
      in it, too?
Do I suspect it's that of which Willa's silence is composed? If so, of what
      is mine composed?
We lie there just a minute, or a year, the surgings and the pulsings in
      my heart and groin
are so intense that finally Paul's forgotten, only Willa's there with me,
      my docile longings.
Willa's turned towards me, her eyes are closed, I bring my face down
      closer, next to hers.
Astonishing that Willa should be in the visible with me, glowing in the
      world of pertinent form.
I move my lips towards hers, I can't resist, only this much, this gently,
      but then, no,
with one subtle shift, the mildest movement of the angle of her brow,
      Willa repositions us
so that my awkwardness makes absurd my plot of our participation in a
      mutual sensual accord.

With what humiliating force I have to understand I'd been suffering an
    unforgivable illusion;
I'd believed that for a little moment Paul had left us, but he'd been there
    all along,
with the unwavering omniscience of a parent, the power of what someday
    I'll call a conscience.
What had ever made me think I'd so easily obliterate him from the fraying
    dusk of childhood?
Weren't we contained in him, held in him; wouldn't fearful heart forever
    now falter in its flight?

The Question

The middle of the night, she's wide awake, carefully lying as far away as
    she can from him.
He turns in his sleep and she can sense him realizing she's not in the
    place she usually is,
then his sleep begins to change, he pulls himself closer, his arm comes
    comfortably around her.
"Are you awake?" she says, then, afraid that he might think she's asking
    him for sex,
she hurries on, "I want to know something; last summer, in Cleveland,
    did you have someone else?"
She'd almost said—she was going to say—"Did you have a *lover?*" but
    she'd caught herself;
she'd been frightened by the word, she realized; it was much too definite,
    at least for now.
Even so, it's only after pausing that he answers, "No," with what feeling
    she can't tell.
He moves his hand on her, then with a smile in his voice asks, "Did
    you have somebody in Cleveland?"
"That's not what I was asking you," she says crossly. "But that's what I
    asked *you,*" he answers.
She's supposed to be content now, the old story, she knows that she's
    supposed to be relieved,
but she's not relieved, her tension hasn't eased the slightest bit, which
    doesn't surprise her.
She's so confused that she can't really even say now if she wants to believe
    him or not.
Anyway, what about that pause? Was it because in the middle of the
    night and six months later
he wouldn't have even known what she was talking about, or was it
    because he needed that moment
to frame an answer which would neutralize what might after all have
    been a shocking thrust
with a reasonable deflection, in this case, his humor: a laugh that's like
    a lie and is.

"When would I have found the time?" he might have said, or, "Who in Cleveland could I love?"

Or, in that so brief instant, might he have been finding a way to stay in the realm of truth,

as she knew he'd surely want to, given how self-righteously he esteemed his ethical integrities?

It comes to her with a start that what she most deeply and painfully suspects him of is a *renunciation.*

She knows that he has no one now; she thinks she knows there's been no contact from Cleveland,

but she still believes that there'd been something then, and if it was as important as she thinks,

it wouldn't be so easily forgotten, it would still be with him somewhere as a sad regret,

perhaps a precious memory, but with that word, renunciation, hooked to it like a price tag.

Maybe that was what so rankled her, that she might have been the object of his charity, his *goodness.*

That would be too much; that he would have wronged her, then sacrificed himself for her.

Yes, "Lover," she should have said it, "Lover, lover," should have made him try to disavow it.

She listens to his breathing; he's asleep again, or has he taught himself to feign that, too?

"No, last summer in Cleveland I didn't have a lover, I have never been to Cleveland, I love you.

There is no Cleveland, I adore you, and, as you'll remember, there was no last summer:

the world last summer didn't yet exist, last summer still was universal darkness, chaos, pain."

Meditation

You must never repeat this to him, *but when I started seeing my guru
was when I got pregnant.*

*I'm not bothered to think there's a connection—we'd been trying so
long—but he would be.*

*He doesn't like my Baba, he says that he's repelled by him; I think he's
really envious.*

*But why? Just because I believe in one person doesn't hurt my feelings for
someone else.*

*You're supposed to give yourself to the guru, that's the whole idea, not
that* way, *though.*

*He makes so much fuss: Baba is a fake, Baba is a pig; he says that I
should leave him,*

*but he knows I won't: if he made me choose, I don't know what I'd do;
and there's the baby.*

*When we made the baby, after my first visit to the ashram, I was so quiet
inside, so serene,*

*as though I'd never been alive before; I felt Baba with me, just like when
I met him.*

*I knew right away the pregnancy had taken, I knew I'd finally get my
child; I was so happy.*

*I'm not lying to him, just not telling him; I can't, I won't. Don't you,
either—promise!*

Politics

They're discussing the political situation they've been watching evolve
in a faraway country.
He's debating intensely, almost lecturing, about fanaticism and religion,
the betrayal of ideals.
He believes he's right, but even as he speaks he knows within himself
that it's all incidental;
he doesn't really care that much, he just can't help himself, what he's
really talking about
is the attraction that he feels she feels towards those dark and passionate
young men
just now glowing on the screen with all the unimpeachable righteousness
of the once-oppressed.
He says that just because they've been afflicted isn't proof against their
lying and conniving.
What he means is that they're not, because she might find them virile,
therefore virtuous.
He says that there are always forces we don't see that use these things for
evil ends.
What he means is that he's afraid that she might turn from him towards
someone suffering,
or, as possible, towards someone who'd share with similar conviction her
abhorrence of suffering.
He means he's troubled by how *sure* she is, how her compassions are so
woven into her identity.
Isn't the degree to which she's certain of her politics, hence of her rightness
in the world,
the same degree to which she'd be potentially willing to risk herself, and
him, and everything?
Also, should she wish to justify an action in her so firmly grounded socio-
ethical system,
any action, concupiscence, promiscuity, orgy, wouldn't it not only let
her but abet her?
Sometimes he feels her dialectics and her assurance are assertions of some
ultimate availability.

Does he really want someone so self-sufficient, who knows herself so
well, knows so much?
In some ways, he thinks—has he really come to this?—he might want
her knowing *nothing*.
No, not nothing, just . . . a little less . . . and with less fervor, greater
pragmatism, realism.
More and more in love with her, touched by her, he still goes on, to his
amazement, arguing.

Pillow Talk

Please try to understand, it was only one small moment, it didn't mean
      a thing, not really.
He was nice enough, but I didn't like him that much, I just felt, you've
      felt it, too, I'm sure,
a burden in my chest, as though I couldn't catch my breath, or get my
      heartbeat straight.
You know, I know you know: there's an ache in you, you want to make
      it stop, that awful flurrying;
you can't get back to where you used to like to be, everything is out of
      balance in you,
and you realize, even if you'd rather not, that the only way is with this
      other person,
you can't tell how you come to that conclusion, you feel silly, you hardly
      even know him,
he's almost not important anyway, he just represents release from all of
      it, a correction,
but you know that nothing else will get this settled in you, that you'll
      always be like this,
with this sense of incompletion, unless you act, even though you might
      not really want to,
so you go ahead and while it's happening you don't think of things like
      evil or betrayal,
you just want your inner world back in order so you can start to live your
      life again,
and then it's over, ended, you won't ever need him anymore, you realize
      it's finished, done.
I thought that you should know, that if you knew you'd understand: tell
      me, do you? Understand?

Ethics

The only time, I swear, I ever fell more than abstractly in love with
      someone else's wife,
I managed to maintain the clearest sense of innocence, even after the
      woman returned my love,
even after she'd left her husband and come down on the plane from
      Montreal to be with me,
I still felt I'd done nothing immoral, that whole disturbing category had
      somehow been effaced;
even after she'd arrived and we'd gone home and gone to bed, and even
      after, the next morning,
when she crossed my room undressed—I almost looked away; we were
      both as shy as adolescents—
and all that next day when we walked, made love again, then slept,
      clinging to each other,
even then, her sleeping hand softly on my chest, her gentle breath gently
      moving on my cheek,
even then, or not until then, not until the new day touched upon us,
      and I knew, knew absolutely,
that though we might love each other, something in her had to have the
      husband, too,
and though she'd tried, and would keep trying to overcome herself, I
      couldn't wait for her,
did that perfect guiltlessness, that sure conviction of my inviolable virtue,
      flee me,
to leave me with a blade of loathing for myself, a disgust with who I
      guessed by now I was,
but even then, when I took her to the airport and she started up that
      corridor the other way,
and we waved, just waved—anybody watching would have thought that
      we were separating friends—
even then, one part of my identity kept claiming its integrity, its non-
      involvement, even chastity,
which is what I castigate myself again for now, not the husband or his
      pain, which he survived,

nor the wife's temptation, but the thrill of evil that I'd felt, then kept
   myself from feeling.

The Mirror

The way these days she dresses with more attention to go out to pass the
    afternoon alone,
shopping or just taking walks, she says, than when they go together to a
    restaurant or party:
it's such a subtle thing, how even speak of it, how imagine he'd be able
    to explain it to her?
The way she looks for such long moments in the mirror as she gets ready,
    putting on her makeup;
the way she looks so deeply at herself, gazes at her eyes, her mouth,
    down along her breasts:
what is he to say, that she's looking at herself in ways he's never seen
    before, more *carnally*?
She would tell him he was mad, or say something else he doesn't want
    no matter what to hear.
The way she puts her jacket on with a flourish, the way she gaily smiles
    going out the door,
the door, the way the door slams shut, the way its latch clicks shut behind
    her so emphatically.
What is he to think? What is he to say, to whom? The mirror, jacket,
    latch, the awful door?
He can't touch the door, he's afraid he'll break the frightening covenant
    he's made with it.
He can't look into the mirror, either, that dark, malicious void: who
    knows what he might see?

The Call

When one of my oldest and dearest friends died and another friend called
to console me,
I found myself crying—I hadn't thought I would—and said, "I didn't
know I'd feel this badly."
Now, a year later, the second friend calls again, this time because his
mistress has left him.
He's anguished, his voice torn; "I didn't know," he tells me, "that I'd
feel this badly."
I'm shocked to hear him use precisely the words I had in my grief, but
of course I understand.
There are more calls, and more, but in the end they all add up to much
the same thing.
The mistress had warned him time and again, if not in so many words,
that this might happen;
she'd asked him to leave his wife, he hadn't yet, but thought his honest
oath to was in effect.
How was he to know that what he'd taken as playful after-intercourse
endearments were threats?
Now that this terrible thing has happened, he's promised he'll really do
it, but too late:
his beloved has found someone else, she's in love, no question now of
beginning over.
At first my friend's desperation is sad to behold, his self-esteem is in
harrowing decline;
decisiveness, or a lack of it, his lack of it, has become the key factor in
his value system.
Gradually, though, he begins to focus on the new lover, on his insip-
idness, his pitiful accomplishments.
There are flaws to this attack, though, because with each new proof of
the other's shortcomings,
with each attempt to neutralize his effectiveness, my friend's self-blame
becomes more acute.
Still, he can't say to himself, "Behold this giant competitor, this (Freud-
ian) father of a man,"

so he keeps diminishing the other, which only augments his sense of the
capriciousness of fate.
Then, to his relief (though he won't quite admit it), he finds sometimes
he's furious at the woman.
How could she have done this? She'd known the risks he'd taken in
doubling his affections,
shouldn't she simply have accepted his ambivalence and hesitation as a
part of their relation?
And what about his wife; yes, some innocence, some purity has been
transgressed there, too.
Her suspicions had been hot; she'd accepted his denials; wasn't that an
offering to the mistress?
Aren't there violations, then, not just of his own good intentions but of
his wife's generosity?
He's often hot with rage now, he doesn't even know at whom, but then
he has to stop himself.
He doesn't want to blame the mistress *too* much, in case she should,
despite all, come back,
and he doesn't want to hate his wife, who still doesn't know, or is even
kinder than he thought.
So he keeps dutifully forgiving everyone, which throws the whole fault
back on him again
and makes him wonder what kind of realignment could possibly redeem
so much despair?
No, it's all ruined in advance, everything is stuck, the only thing he can
do now is forget.
They're so degrading, these issues which can be resolved by neither
consolation nor forgiveness.
No wonder my friend would cast his misery as mourning; no wonder,
biting my tongue, I'd let him.

The Image

She began to think that jealousy was only an excuse, a front, for something
    even more rapacious,
more maniacally pathological in its readiness to sacrifice its own well-
    being for its satisfaction.
Jealousy was supposed to be a fact of love, she thought, but this was a
    compulsion, madness,
it didn't have a thing to do with love, it was perfectly autonomous, love
    was just its vehicle.
She thought: wasn't there a crazy hunger, even a delight, in how he'd
    pounced on her betrayal?
There hadn't even *been* betrayal until he'd made it so; for her, before
    that, it had been a whim,
a frivolity she'd gone to for diversion, it hadn't had anything to do with
    him, or them.
Her apologies meant nothing, though, nor her fervent promise of re-
    pentance, he *held* his hurt,
he cultivated, stroked it, as though that was all that kept him in rela-
    tionship with her.
He wanted her to think she'd maimed him: what was driving him to such
    barbarous vindictiveness?
She brought to mind a parasite, waiting half a lifetime for its victim to
    pass beneath its branch,
then coming to fully sentient, throbbing, famished life and without hes-
    itation letting go.
It must have almost starved in him, she thinks, all those years spent
    scenting out false stimuli,
all that passive vigilance, secreting bitter enzymes of suspicion, ingesting
    its own flesh;
he must have eaten at himself, devouring his own soul until his chance
    had finally come.
But now it had and he had driven fangs in her and nothing could contain
    his terrible tenacity.
She let the vision take her further; they had perished, both of them, there
    they lay, decomposing,

39

one of them drained white, the other bloated, gorged, stale blood oozing
through its carapace.
Only as a stupid little joke, she thought, would anybody watching dare
wonder which was which.

The Idyll

I just don't want to feel put down; if she decides she wants to sleep with
    someone, listen,
great, go ahead, but I want to know about it and I want the other guy
    to know I know;
I don't want some mother sliming in her sack, using her and thinking he's
    one up me.

She's always touching men, she sort of leans at them, she has to have
    them notice her,
want to grab her: it's like she's always telling me she's on the lookout for
    some stud,
some gigantic sex-machine who's going to get it on with her a hundred
    times an hour.

Once it really happened: she looked me in the eye and said, "I balled
    someone else last night."
Christ, I felt these ridges going up and down my jaw, I thought my teeth
    were going to break.
What'd I do? I took her home, we made out like maniacs. What else was
    I supposed to do?

Sometimes I wonder if I need it. I mean, she'll be coming onto somebody,
    as usual,
I'll want to crack her head for her, but if I think about it, I might get a
    buzz from it,
it must be what going into battle's like: sometimes I think going nuts from
    her is my religion.

I don't know if she fools around much now; I guess I'm not a whole lot
    into other women either.
The last time I was with another chick—she was a little knockout, too—
    I wasn't hardly there.
I realized who I wanted to be with was her. I turned off. Hell, is that
    how you get faithful?

The Silence

He hasn't taken his eyes off you since we walked in, although you seem
    not to notice particularly.
Only sometimes, when your gaze crosses his, mightn't it leave a very
    tiny *tuft* behind?
It's my imagination surely, but mightn't you be all but imperceptibly
    acknowledging his admiration?
We've all known these things; the other, whom we've never seen before,
    but whose ways we recognize,
and with whom we enter into brilliant complicities; soul's receptors tuned
    and armed;
the concealed messages, the plots, the tactics so elegant they might have
    been rehearsed:
the way we wholly disregard each other, never, except at the most casually
    random intervals,
let our scrutinies engage, but then that deep, delicious draft, that eager
    passionate appreciation . . .
I tell myself that I don't care, as I might not sometimes, when no rival's
    happened by,
but I do care now, I care acutely, I just wonder what the good would be
    if I told you I can see
your mild glances palpably, if still so subtly, furtively, intertwining now
    with his?
I'd only be insulting you, violating my supposed trust in you, belittling
    both of us.
We've spent so much effort all these years learning to care for one
    another's sensitivities.
In an instant that's all threatened; your affections seem as tenuous as
    when we met,
and I have to ask myself, are you more valuable to me the more that
    you're at risk?
Am I to you? It's degrading, thinking we're more firmly held together by
    our mutual anxiety.
If my desire is susceptible to someone else's valuations of its object, then
    what am I?

Can I say that my emotions are my own if in my most intimate affection
such contaminations lurk?
Still, though, what if this time I'd guessed right, and what if I should try
to tell you,
to try to laugh about it with you, to use our union, and our hard-earned
etiquettes to mock him,
this intruder—look—who with his dream of even daring to attempt you
would be ludicrous?
There would still be risks I almost can't let myself consider: that you'd
be humoring me,
that the fierce intensity of your attraction to him would already constitute
a union with him,
I'd be asking you to lie and doing so you'd be thrown more emphatically
into his conspiracy;
your conniving with him would relegate me to the status of an obligation,
a teary inconvenience.
This is so exhausting: when will it relent? It seems never, not as long as
consciousness exists.
Therefore, as all along I knew I would, as I knew I'd have to, I keep still,
conceal my sorrow.
Therefore, when you ask, "Is something wrong?" what is there to answer
but, "Of course not, why?"

Soliloquies

1

Strange that sexual jealousy should be so much like sex itself: the same engrossing reveries,
the intricate, voluptuous pre-imaginings, the impatient plottings towards a climax, then climax . . .
Or, not quite climax, since jealousy is different in how uninvolved it is in consummation.
What is its consummation but negation? Not climax but relief, a sigh of resignation, disappointment.
Still, how both depend upon a judicious intermingling of the imaginary and the merely real,
and how important image is for both, the vivid, breath-held unscrolling of fugitive inner effigies.
Next to all our other minds, how pure both are, what avid concentration takes us in them.
Maybe this is where jealousy's terrific agitation comes from, because, in its scalding focus,
a desperate single-mindedness is imposed upon the soul and the sad, conditioned soul responds,
so fervently, in such good faith, it hardly needs the other person for its delicious fever.
Is there anything in life in which what is fancied is so much more intense than what's accomplished?
We know it's shadow, but licentious consciousness goes on forever manufacturing . . . fever.

2

The stupidity of it, the repetitiveness, the sense of all one's mental mechanisms run amok.
Knowing that pragmatically, statistically, one's fantasies are foolish, but still being trapped.

The almost unmanageable foreboding that one's character won't be up to its own exigencies.

Knowing one is one's own victim; how self-diminishing to have to ask, "Who really *am* I, then?"

I am someone to be rescued from my mind, but the agent of my suffering is its sole redemption;

only someone else, a specific someone else, can stop me from inflicting this upon myself.

And so within myself, in this unsavory, unsilent solitude of self, I fall into an odious dependency.

I'm like an invalid relying absolutely on another's rectitude; but the desperate invalid, abandoned,

would have at least the moral compensation of knowing that he wasn't doing this to himself;

philosophically, his reliance would be limited by the other's sense of obligation, or its absence.

This excruciating, groundless need becomes more urgent, more to be desired the more it's threatened,

while its denouement promises what one still believes will be an unimaginably luxurious release.

3

I try to imagine the kind of feeling which would come upon me if I really were betrayed now.

How long would I remain in that abject state of mind? When would it end? Am I sure it would?

What constitutes a state of mind at all? Certain chunks of feeling, of pleasure or pain?

I postulate the pain, but can I really? My mood prevents it. Is that all I am, then, mood?

Sometimes I feel firmly socketed within myself; other moments, I seem barely present.

Which should I desire? Mightn't it be better not to feel anything if I'm helpless anyway?

I try to reconceive the problem: I am he who will forgive his being wronged, but can I know I will?

All my mind will tell me absolutely and obsessively is that its future isn't
     in my governance.
Might that be why the other's possible offense seems much more *rank*
     than mine would ever be?
My betrayal would be whimsical, benign, the hymen of my innocence
     would be quickly reaffirmed.
Hers infects, contaminates, is ever the first premeditated step of some
     squalid longer term.
I would forgive, but suspect that she might already be beyond forgiveness:
     whose fault then?

4

What would be the difference? The way jealousy seeps into my notions
     of intention and volition,
the annihilating force it has: mightn't it be grounded in the furies of more
     radical uncertainty?
That nothing lasts, that there's no real reason why it doesn't last, and
     that there's death,
and more maddening still that existence has conjectured possibilities of
     an after-death,
but not their certainty, rather more the evidence that any endlessness is
     mental fiction.
And that there might be a God, a potentially beloved other who *would*
     know, this, and everything,
who already has sufficient knowledge of our fate to heal us but may well
     decide not to do so.
How not rage, how, in love, with its promises of permanence, the only
     answer to these doubts,
not find absurd that this, too, should suffer from foreboding, and one so
     mechanically averted?
Might jealousy finally suggest that what we're living isn't ever what we
     think we are?
What, though, would more require our love, our being loved, our vow
     of faithfulness and faith?
And what would more compel that apprehensive affirmation: *I'll love you
     forever, will you me?*

3

She, Though

Her friend's lover was dying, or not "friend," they weren't that yet, if
      they ever really were;
it was another girl she'd found to share the studio she'd rented in an old
      commercial building.
Both of them were painters, the other serious, hardworking, she floun-
      dering and unconfident.
She gave you the feeling people fresh from art school often do that the
      painter's life
would be just fine except for all those hours you had to put in with the
      bothersome canvas.
"Lover" isn't quite the right word, either: the couple were too young,
      "boyfriend" would be better,
although, given the strenuousness of their trial, the more grownup term
      could well apply.
He was twenty-three or -four, a physicist who'd already done his doctorate
      and published papers;
he had cancer of the brain; it had only recently been diagnosed but the
      news had all been bad.
I forget exactly how I met them: there weren't that many writers or artists
      in our city then,
we mostly knew each other, even if our fellowship seemed more grounded
      in proximity than sympathy.
She and I, I suppose I should say, once almost had a thing; she asked
      me to sit for her,
and when she'd posed me and was fussing with her charcoal, I understood
      why I was really there.
I was surprised; though we'd known each other for a while we were casual
      friends at best,
we'd never expressed attraction for each other, and I remember feeling
      sometimes that she resented me.
I had a reputation as a worker, even if I hadn't published anything except
      some book reviews
and a criticism of an art show, but she may have felt I had more prestige
      than I should have.

49

I had nothing particularly against her; maybe the tenuousness of her involvement in her work

and what it represented to me of myself made her less attractive than she might have been.

I distrusted her, wasn't sure why she wanted me, but wasn't anyway about to get in bed.

Her signaling was pretty raw: she'd take my head in her hands to move me to a new position,

then hold me longer than she had to, and she'd look intently *in* my eyes instead of at them.

Finally she just said, "Let's do it," but I turned her down, in a way which at the time

I thought was very bright but which may certainly have had to do with how badly things turned out.

I told her that I liked her but that I could only sleep with girls I loved, really loved.

She accepted my refusal in the spirit I'd hoped she would, as an example of my inner seriousness,

and as also having to do—through I don't recall what track—with my dedication as an artist.

That dedication, or obsession, or semblance of obsession, counted for much in those days.

For most of us it was all we had, struggling through our perplexed, interminable apprenticeships.

We were trying to create identities as makers and as thinkers, and that entailed so much.

I never realized until lately just how traumatic the project of my own self-remaking was.

I wreaked such violence on myself; the frivolous, not unsuccessful adolescent I had been

had to be remolded from such contradictory clues as I could find into a wholly other person.

I'd been an *athlete*, for heaven's sake, I'd been a party boy, I hung out, I drank, I danced:

one New Year's Eve I'd set out to kiss a hundred girls, and nearly had; that kind of thing.

Now who was I? Someone sitting hours on end going crazy looking at an empty piece of paper.

Everything I'd learned in college seemed garbled and absurd: I knew
     nothing about anything.
All I understood was that I wasn't ready for this yet, that I'd have to reach
     some higher stage
before I'd have the right to even think that I was someone who could
     call himself a poet.
We must have all felt more or less like that, though it seemed important
     never to admit it.
"Morally perfect yourself, then you'll write a poem," I read somewhere
     not long ago: is it true?
I don't think I know yet, I surely didn't then, but that was what we'd
     somehow come to,
a mix of saint and genius, neither of which we ever in our wildest ravings
     dreamed we'd be.
Maybe that was why we liked extremities so much, and mental dramas;
     we spoke forever about *limits*,
things like microcosm-macrocosm, or the way the solar system and atomic
     model seemed to match:
probably we thought that, on that wide a scale, we'd at least be sure of
     being *somewhere*.
We loved it when things went so far they turned into their opposites; the
     courteous criminal,
the rake who in his single-minded lust achieves a sanctity, the cabalist
     obscene with bliss.
There were always remnants of religion in our schemes; somehow from
     the mishmash of our education
we'd decided that you didn't practice art for its own sake or even to be
     competent or famous;
it was all supposed to be a part of a something that would lift you to
     another realm,
another mode of being, where you'd attain the "absolute"—a word we
     loved—along with "mystic."
But there was even more than that; art was going to be the final word
     on all else, too:
morality, philosophy, religion; if there was a God, wasn't He the God of
     Dante or Bach,
rather than a theologian's or a prophet's, unless they dreamed their vi-
     sions, too, in poetry?

51

When we thought of social issues or of politics, it was always with as
   audacious an immoderation.
"Justice" meant the universe of justice; the ideal, platonic shape, some-
   thing in your soul
that mirrored an imaginary, perfect state, at which the particulars of real
   life could only hint.
History for us was the history of arts and letters, anything of moment was
   attached to that.
So young we were; we had theories about everything, life, the soul: Did
   art spring from neurosis?
Was its insanity redemptive? Were you damned by art, exalted? It all
   depended on the day.
But being young wasn't the whole problem; there was moral character
   to be considered, too.
That girl, for instance, in that enormous studio: it irritated me the way
   she'd waste her time,
puttering, reading magazines; she spent more effort sending slides to
   galleries than painting.
She'd been in some group exhibitions—she wasn't without talent—now
   she'd convinced herself
that being "professional" meant not picking up a brush unless a dealer
   promised you a show.
I knew all that was posturing, self-deception, sham; I knew from what I
   went through myself
how repugnant working was when you didn't know if there was ever going
   to be a recompense.
I don't mean to make light of it, what we were trying to do was hard,
   and not just the work,
in some ways that was easy: what was really difficult was waiting for the
   labor to begin;
you had to tell yourself every minute that you did it why you did and
   what it was for.
So little really happened, and no one but a friend or two even noticed
   what you were doing.
The dropout rate among us was impressive: over time so many drifted
   off, some to law school,
some into endless therapies; a black sculptor began to drink and disap-
   peared into the ghetto;

someone else became an "art consultant," choosing prints and paintings
for corporate boardrooms.
It did seem easier for some, though; some were seen as having been
successful from the start.
I suppose it had to do with confidence; they weren't necessarily the ones
who'd won the prizes,
but they seemed certified, legitimized, they had clues about their ultimate
trajectories;
you felt they'd freed themselves from thinking they were being *watched*,
those chosen few,
they were on their own and, though they hadn't done much yet, were
envied and looked up to.
What happens to those younger masters isn't always happy; maybe that
much unquestioning admiration,
that much carrying of so many other people's hopes, even at that level,
isn't good for you.
Also, when everyone's that young, there's much misreading of charisma
and eccentricity as talent.
Some, anyway, would turn out to have the gift, but not enough of what
you could call the *cunning*,
the kind of objectivity artists seem to need to keep their work evolving
in meaningful ways.
They'd find a mode of doing what their gift had offered them, then stay
with it too long,
and find later that they'd used it up and gotten stuck in some too flashy
segment of themselves.
Others would have the cunning, and the drive it seemed to go with, but
too much of it;
they'd become impatient, and move off to something close to art—usually
involving money—
to which they'd bring their ingenuity and energy, becoming rich or
celebrated, but so what?
She, I don't have to say, wasn't one of the elect, no more than I'd dare
claim I was.
The other girl may have been; if so, she controlled the arrogance it
sometimes went with.
The boyfriend for all we knew was a genius; we had to take his mysterious
accomplishments on faith.

He was brilliant enough in conversation, at any rate, and had an attractive
    calm about him.
In the face of his illness, and though no one dared speak of it, his at
    least possible death,
the two of them had evolved one of those surprising complicities of
    resignation and acceptance
which can take the most unexceptional people at such times, and they
    were hardly unexceptional.
They had an admirably mature relationship; they respected and encour-
    aged one another's work,
and were solicitous towards each other in gentle, complicated ways the
    rest of us found heartening.
But with all that, the dignity they seemed committed to achieving now
    was of another order.
For one thing, there was no denial in it, no trying to behave more fittingly
    before the facts.
They stayed mostly to themselves, and worked; if they did go anywhere,
    to an opening, say,
they left early, refusing to let anything intrude on their resolute and by
    now ennobling composure.
The rest of us must have been a little awed; being with them was like
    being with a movie star.
We may have been excited, too, and secretly inspired, but all they seemed
    to want from us
was that we act as though nothing unusual was happening, and we were
    all too happy to comply.
She, though, once she'd found out about it—the girl apparently at first
    had kept it from her—
wasn't taking anything so calmly, wasn't having any of this stoicism, this
    holding back.
I don't know how, but she was all at once their chum, their confidante,
    their social secretary.
She was blazing with consideration for them, some unsuspected energy
    had been released in her.
She dropped her painting altogether now, and did good deeds for them
    instead: she was everywhere,
organizing quiet dinners, getting people to throw parties; she even once
    promoted a recital,

which was supposed to give some of our musicians an opportunity to
    play but which she turned—
and not in an unpleasantly pretentious way—into an elegant soiree and
    cocktail honoring them.
They became, in fact, as she took over, the unofficial guests of honor
    everywhere they went.
They hardly seemed to notice, though, and to hardly notice her; she was
    like a stage director,
rushing back and forth behind the scenes, keeping all the action moving
    unobtrusively along,
except it wasn't the audience which was supposed to be oblivious of all
    the cable-hauling,
the changing sets and lighting, but the innocent creatures out on the
    apron of the stage.
I often wondered, considering what they seemed to have wanted before
    she started in on that,
whether they were ever bothered by her benevolent chicanery; they didn't
    appear to be.
They could have stopped her, but their sorrow may have been more
    oppressive than we knew;
maybe there was something that they needed after all, maybe it was just
    that much attention.
Or it could all have been just another factor to be balanced in their
    brilliant equation,
the way one of their mother's clutching a tissue to an irrepressible tear
    would have been.
If they didn't have a problem with her machinations, though, I did; I
    found it all depressing.
I thought I knew what she was up to—a naked compensation for her
    failures at the easel—
and I began to stay away from functions she was overseeing, which meant
    most of them by now.
I just kept to myself more, even if it meant afflicting myself with still
    more loneliness,
a loneliness the opposite of what I found in books, where you went off
    on your holy pilgrimage,
enriched yourself with arcane meditations on the universe, and then
    produced your masterpiece.

My masterpiece, if I still could have a fantasy of such a thing, seemed
     more buried every day
beneath the layers of confusion, uncertainty, and mental maladroitness
     to which I was so susceptible.
I don't remember what finally brought me to the party where I saw the
     three of them again.
It was just a night at someone's house; everyone was there, I was glad to
     be there, too,
hearing other people's voices, breathing other people's breath, feeling
     ordinary human warmth.
The young man still looked well enough, the two of them were sitting
     at the piano, whispering.
She was near them; when she saw me, she came over, she was glad to
     see me, where had I been?
There was something she'd been wanting to ask me; no, not right now,
     wait, later on.
I couldn't conceive what question she might have for me, but I'd been
     by myself so much
that any contact was intriguing, and besides, she looked, with her new
     glow of purpose, quite enchanting.
As the party swirled on, I watched her; it was remarkable how she'd
     involved herself with them.
I'd never thought of her as subtle but I had to recognize how much
     intelligence she had for this.
She was always near them, but never overbearingly so; she was just
     available to them,
they were always in a triangle with her, as though she possessed some
     benign, proprietary power.
She'd bring them drinks and sandwiches, lead people over to them, lean
     down to listen, laugh.
It seemed natural when she'd lightly touch the lover's shoulder, or stroke
     the girl's hair.
Later on, I caught her hand and led her to the bedroom; what had she
     been going to ask?
What she asked was if I knew anything to read on death; could I rec-
     ommend a book on death.
At first I didn't understand what she was saying, I couldn't register it, get
     it down.

What? "You've read a lot of books," she said. "I need one to give to
     somebody who's dying."
She said it quietly, she was serious, almost solemn, but she was looking
     at my eyes this time.
"Something to comfort them," she added with conspiratorial intensity,
     "in their ordeal."
I don't remember what I answered, if I did—I may have said they're all
     on death, all books,
I still believed it sometimes in those days, it sometimes seemed the core
     of my aesthetic code.
What I'm hearing now is "Timor mortis conturbat me"—"The fear of
     death is killing me"—
but what I remember thinking then, with a desperate conviction, was
     that she'd beaten me:
she'd held her grudge this long, and then attacked, prevailed, and won
     our little agon.
By assuming, or making believe that she assumed, I'd be so unaware of
     something of such moment,
she'd let me know I was an outcast among outcasts, subtracted from what
     society I had, a pretender,
and by turning my own medium against me, showing how absurd it
     would have been for me to think
that writing could heal or solace real grief, she'd proved that my preten-
     sions were a farce.
I think I was amazed that she'd have used her own good deeds to get at
     me, but more importantly,
I knew she'd touched some truth, and that something in me had been
     undermined so profoundly
that as I turned from her, although of course I wouldn't let her know, I
     must have almost staggered.
I think I doubted even then, though, how much my psychic storm really
     had to do with her.
I knew she didn't hate me *that* much, and that what had happened to
     us wasn't very deep.
No, it wasn't me she'd hated and wanted vengeance from, it was *art*; I
     was just the medium,
a handy means to rebel against art, to degrade it, express how much she
     despised it.

57

She'd chosen me to use—and this *had* hurt—because she knew I knew
    I wasn't really pure.
All my narcissism, all the juvenile self-indulgence that had let me think
    that as I was
I could still be an initiate in art's exalted realm, no matter how I lied
    and twisted my identity,
she'd long ago intuited, and finally struck with, and she may have even
    guessed—I hope not—
that in this moment I was living out what in turning to a life by art I'd
    been trying to evade.
I don't think I cared if she was taking satisfaction from my turmoil, she
    didn't matter anymore.
I beheld myself, and I was mortified, not because of anybody else's ideas
    or norms or values,
but for my own, all I'd studied and prepared for, which had suddenly
    become shameful to me.
"You must change your life": I knew Rilke's line already, now I had a
    hint of how it happened.
It's not easy to remember how much of what I later came to understand
    revealed itself that evening:
a mass of sad intention was set under way in me I've spent all these years
    trying to enact.
Right then I was most likely struck by just the wrongness of how I'd so
    far conceived my task.
I'd believed that art was everything, the final resolution of all my insecurity
    and strivings.
Now I realized that in attempting to create a character in art, someone
    who would live for art,
I'd turned away from something in myself, some lapse I hadn't glimpsed,
    and, more shocking still,
I knew that architecture, poetry, and painting weren't the self-containing
    glories I'd imagined,
but that they, too, could have evasions lurking in them, grievous cosmic
    flinchings from reality.
Art wasn't everything, nothing could be everything, but more crucially,
    art *needed* you:
I knew now that if you hated art, as she did, that was what you hated in
    it, that responsibility,

not to making up a self which might someday be worthy of ecstasy or
fame, but to art itself,
to the negating force it could become unless you understood what its
decisive limits were.
The power, the willed resolve I'd believed you needed for your work, I
knew now were elementary,
that arduous and obscure responsibility was what mattered most, and I
intuited, and *knew*,
that what it consisted of was a concern, for all of us, for every human
being: one by one.
The forms and substances were incidental, *we* were form and substance;
subject, object, reason.
"You must change your life." I knew then, or began to know, that what
art needed at the end
was an acceptance of what's muddled and confused in us, what's broken
by our lives and living.
To love art meant to love our errors; what we owed art was ourselves and
our imperfect world.
"Timor mortis conturbat me." "You must change your life." I was left
with my forbidding mottoes,
my attempts to overcome my unconfidence and indolence, and every
day my sorry stabs at poems.
Whether I used well what I learned that night, or if it changed me, how
am I to know?
Can we ever say in all good conscience we've really changed? We only
have our single story.
In mine, the physicist, the young man, the boy—what else would I think
he was by now?—
the poor boy dies sooner even than predicted; this all takes place in just
some months.
The boy dies, the girlfriend moves away; I see her work reviewed, years
later, in the *Times*;
they loved her: she was praised especially for her "mastery of expression":
good for her.
She—how specify her now? my antagonist? my demon other? the an-
tithesis in my groping dialectic?—
she drops from sight: I forgave her, but never heard another breath about
her, and never wanted to.

4

A Dream of Mind

for Adam Zagajewski

The Method

A dream of method first, in which mind is malleable, its products as
    revisable as sentences,
in which I'll be able to extract and then illuminate the themes of being
    as I never have.
I'm intrigued—how not be?—but I soon realize that though so much
    flexibility is tempting—
whole zones of consciousness wouldn't only be reflected or referred to,
    but embodied, as themselves,
before the sense-stuff of the world is attached to them, adulterating and
    misrepresenting them—
I have only the sketchiest notion of how to incorporate this exotic and
    complicated methodology,
and when I try, something in my character resists manipulating elements
    of mind so radically.
Imagine being offered an instrument to play that violated all your previous
    aesthetic norms,
with a fleshy, tender, sensitive component, crudely sewn or soldered to
    an innocently inorganic,
and a shape that hinted at the most contradictory techniques—brute
    force, a delicate dexterity.
You know you're supposed to draw this hybrid to your breast, to try to
    coax from it its music,
but under the tension of so many formal contradictions, what actually
    would you bring forth?
Isn't this like that? I'd be dreaming dreams of dreams, hammering out
    ideas of dreams:
wouldn't anything I'd come up with have to be a monstrous mix of
    substance and intention?
Making something out of nothing; surely more than matters of order or
    proportion are at stake.
I feel myself go cold now, taken by a clarity that makes me ask if I'm
    not already in the dream,
if I'm not merely being tempted by it, in the sense that one is tempted
    by an ill desire.

What if all this theory's the equivalent of nightmare, its menace mas-
    querading as philosophy?
Can mind contort itself so recklessly and not endanger its most basic links
    to common sense?
I dream a dream of method, comprehending little of the real forces or
    necessities of dream,
and find myself entangled in the dream, entrapped, already caught in
    what the dream contrived,
in what it made, of my ambitions, or of what it itself aspired to for its
    darker dreaming.

Shadows

They drift unobtrusively into the dream, they linger, then they depart,
    but they emanate, always,
an essence of themselves, an aura, of just the frequency my mind needs
    to grasp and contain them.
Sometimes, though, the identity that I sense there, the person I feel
    intimated or implied,
is so fluid and changes so rapidly and dramatically that often I hardly
    know who I'm with.
Someone is there, then they're someone from another moment of my
    life, or even a stranger.
At first I find such volatile mutability surprisingly less agitating than I'd
    have thought,
probably because these others brought and taken away by the dream
    manifest such careless unconcern.
Before long, though, I feel apprehensive: I find that whenever someone
    in the dream changes,
I subtly alter who I am as well, so as to stay in a proper relation with
    this new arrival
who may already be somebody else, someone for whom the self I've come
    up with is obsolete.
Suddenly I'm never quite who I should be; beset by all this tenuous
    veering and blurring,
my character has become the function of its own revisions; I'm a bystander
    in my own dream.
Even my response to such flux is growing unstable; until now I've con-
    sidered it speculatively,
but what says I'm not going to stay in this epistemologically tremulous
    state forever?
I find I'm trying to think how to stop this, but trying to think in dream
    means, as always,
trying to *do*, and what do now with this presence moving towards me,
    wavering, shifting,
now being itself, now another, webbed now in the shadows of memory,
    now brilliant, burning?

Am I to try to engage it, or turn back to myself to steel myself in a more pure concentration?

Even as I watch, it transfigures again; I see it, if it is it, as through ice, or a lens.

I feel a breath touch me now, but is it this breath I feel or someone's I haven't met yet,

is it a whisper I hear or the murmur of multitudes sensing each other closer within me?

How even tell who I am now, how know if I'll ever be more than the field of these interchangings?

Vocations

Blocks of time fall upon me, adhere for a moment, then move astonish-
      ingly away, fleeting, dissolving,
but still I believe that these parcels of experience have a significance
      beyond their accumulation,
that though they bear no evident relation besides being occasionally
      adjacent to each other,
they can be considered in a way that implies consequence, what I come
      to call the dream's "meaning."
Although I can't quite specify how this ostensible meaning differs from
      the sum of its states,
it holds an allure, *solutions* are implied, so I keep winding the dream's
      filaments onto its core.
The problem is that trying to make the recalcitrant segments of the dream
      cohere is distracting;
my mind is always half following what happens while it's half involved
      in this other procedure.
Also, my ideas about meaning keep sending directives into the dream's
      already crowded circuits,
and soon I'm hard put keeping the whole intractable mechanism moving
      along smoothly enough
to allow me to believe that at least I'm making a not overly wasteful use
      of my raw materials.
Although, doesn't the notion of "use" seem questionable, too? Use
      how, and to what end?
To proliferate more complexities when I haven't come to terms with those
      I've already proposed?
Mightn't all of this be only a part of the mind's longing to be other or
      more than it is?
Sometimes I think I'd be better off letting the dream make its own way
      without butting in so,
but no, I understand the chaos I might wreak if I left off these indispens-
      able cohesions.
How depressing dream can feel now, nothing in it can move, everything
      is suspended, waiting,

or, worse, not waiting, going on as it's always gone on but with such
fearful, timid resolve
that I begin to wonder if all that keeps me going is my fear of randomness,
regression, chance.
It doesn't matter anymore: whatever dream meant once, whatever it might
come to mean,
I know the only way I'll ever finish with this anguish is to understand it,
and to understand
was what the dream promised, and what, with all its blundering hopes,
it promises still.

The Solid

Although I'm apparently alone, with a pleasant but unextraordinary feel-
    ing of self-sufficiency,
I know I'm actually a part of a group of people who for reasons the dream
    never makes clear
are unavailable to any of my senses, though I'm always aware of the
    pressure of their presence.
No matter what else I'm doing, no matter how scant the attention I pay,
    I know they're there,
only my response to being in relation with beings I can only imagine
    alters now and again.
Usually I'm comforted: this intuition seems to impart to the dream such
    stability as it has.
Immersed with my mysterious companions in an enormous, benign,
    somehow consoling solid,
all that's required is that I not carelessly set jolts out into that sensitive
    bulk of otherness.
At other, nearly simultaneous moments, I feel signals sent, intentionally
    or not, I can't tell,
which arrive to my consciousness as an irritation, almost an abrasion of
    the material of thought.
In some far corner of dream, someone wants, needs, with such vehement,
    unreasonable fervor,
that even from here I'm afflicted with what I can only believe is an
    equivalent chagrin.
I try to think of ways to send back if not reassurance then an acknowl-
    edgment of my concern,
but I realize this would require not only energy and determination but
    a discernment, a delicacy,
the mere thought of which intimidates me, reinforcing the sense I have
    of my ineffectiveness.
I begin to be afraid then, the dream is deteriorating; how vulnerable I
    am in my very connections.
Don't my worst anxieties rise out of just such ambiguous feelings of
    communion and debt?

I'm suddenly swamped, overwhelmed in these tangles of unasked-for
      sympathies and alliances.
Always then, though, through an operation whose workings I'm never
      forced to explain to myself,
I'm released, the limits of my selfhood are reestablished, the nascent
      nightmare subsides,
and I'm able to reassume the not-incongruous sense of being alone and
      with so many others,
with nothing asked of me more than what any reasonable dream needs
      for its reasonable dreaming,
and the most minor qualms as to what I may have traded for my peace
      of mind, and what lost.

The Charge

An insistence in dream on a succession of seemingly urgent but possibly
   purposeless tasks
to be executed for no evident reason beyond the tautological one that
   dream says they must.
The nature of these undertakings is unclear, imprecise, they can even
   change definition,
I can never find more than the most ambiguous grounds to justify my
   obsession with them.
It seems sometimes that far away in the past of the dream a shameful
   error was committed,
and that these obligations are only my share of a more general rectification
   or atonement.
Often I can't tell if what I'm doing is by any sane measure what I'm
   supposed to be doing,
or whether all my efforts are the groundwork for yet another, still more
   illogical dream.
I'm never unaware either that I'm squandering time; this undermines my
   self-assurance still more,
so, the dream still driving me through it, me still helplessly driving myself
   through the dream,
I begin to think that persisting in this will put me into a state of such
   unmanageable consternation
that everything in me will simply go awry, leaving me tearing at myself
   in rages of frustration.
How long this has been under way, I can't tell; forever, it seems, all the
   time of the dream,
but maybe because I've looked back now, it comes to me that even should
   these needs be satisfied,
their compulsions slaked, it won't have been my doing: dream will just
   have pitied me,
given me surcease, not the satisfaction I'd anticipated despite all, but
   deflection and distraction.
All I'm left to hope for is that something other than nostalgia or regret
   awaits me,

that I won't end up longing for my labors, yearning for the solaces of
    goals I'd never grasped,
trying to remember when the dream of finishing what can't be finished
    ended, or if it did.

The Crime

Violence in the dream, violation of body and spirit; torment, mutilation, butchery, debasement.

At first it hardly feels real, there's something ceremonial in it, something of the dance.

The barbarisms seem formulaic, restrained, they cast a stillness about them, even a calm.

Then it comes once again, the torment, the debasement, and I have to accept that it's real.

Human beings are tearing each other to pieces, their rancor is real, and so is their pain.

Violence in the dream, but I still think—something wants me to think —there are *reasons*:

ideas are referred to, ideals, propositions of order, hierarchies, mores, structures of value.

Even in dream, though, I know it's not true, I know that if reasons there are, they're ill reasons.

Even in dream, I'm ashamed, and then, though I'm frightened, I steel myself and protest.

I protest, but the violence goes on, I cry out, but the pain, the rage, the rancor continue.

Then I suddenly realize I've said nothing at all, what I dreamed was spoken wasn't at all.

I dreamed I protested, I dreamed I cried out: I was mute, there was only an inarticulate moan.

What deceived me to think I'd objected when really I'd only cowered, embraced myself, moaned?

My incompetent courage deceived me, my too-timid hopes for the human, my qualms, my doubts.

Besides the suspicion perhaps that the dream doesn't reveal the horror but draws it from itself,

that dream's truth is its violence, that its pity masks something I don't want to find there.

What I hear now in the dream is the dream lamenting, its sorrow, its fear, its cry.

Caught in the reasons of dream, I call out; caught in its sorrow, I know who I hear cry.

Shells

Shells of fearful insensitivity that I keep having to disadhere from my
    heart, how dream you?
How dream away these tireless reflexes of self-protection that almost define
    heart
and these sick startles of shame at confronting again the forms of fear the
    heart weaves,
the certitudes and the hatreds, the thoughtless fortifications of scarred,
    fearful self?
How dream you, heart hiding, how dream the products of heart foul
    with egotism and fear?
Heart's dream, the spaces holding you are so indistinct and the hurt place
    you lurk so tender,
that even in dream membranes veil and distort you, only fancy and
    falsehood hint where you are.
How can I dream the stripping away of the petrified membranes muffling
    the tremulous heart?
I reach towards the heart and attain only heart's stores of timidity, self-
    hatred, and blame;
the heart which I don't dare bring to my zone of knowledge for fear it
    will shame me again,
afflict me again with its pettiness, coyness, its sham zeal, false pity, and
    false pride.
Dream of my heart, am I only able to dream illusions of you that touch
    me with pity or pride?
How dream the heart's sorrow to redeem what it contains beyond its self-
    defense and disdain?
How forgive heart when the part of me that beholds heart swells so in
    its pride and contempt?
Trying to dream the dream of the heart, I hide myself from it, I veil my
    failures and shame.
Heart, ever unworthy of you, lost in you, will I ever truly dream you,
    or dream beyond you?

Room

I wanted to take up room. What a strange dream! I wanted to take up as
    much room as I could,
to swell up, enlarge, crowd into a corner all the others in the dream with
    me, but why?
Something to do with love, it felt like, but what love needs more volume
    than it has?
Lust, then: its limitlessness, the lure of its ineluctable renewal—but this
    came before lust.
Fear? Yes, the others were always more real than I was, more concrete,
    emphatic: why not fear?
Though I knew that this was my dream, they were the given and I the
    eccentric, wobbling variable.
A dubious plasma, drifting among them, self-consciously sidling, flowing,
    ebbing among them,
no wonder my atoms would boil, trying to gel, and no wonder I'd some-
    times resent them,
brood on them, trying to understand what they were, what my connection
    to them really was.
Sometimes I'd think the point of the dream was to find what of me was
    embodied in them.
What I was with them, though, what they finally were in themselves, I
    hardly could tell.
Sometimes they seemed beasts; I could see them only as beasts, captives
    of hunger and fear.
Sometimes they were angels, nearly on fire, embracing, gleaming with
    grace, gratitude, praise.
But when their lips touched, were they kissing, or gnawing the warmth
    from a maw?
So much threatening pain to each other, so much pain accomplished:
    no surprise I'd think beasts.
But still, I loved them; I wasn't just jealous of them, I loved them, was
    of them, and, more,
I'd grown somehow to know in the dream that part of my love meant
    accounting for them.

Account for them: how, though, why? Did they account for each other, would they for me?

That wasn't what the dream meant to be now; I loved them, I wasn't to ask if they loved me.

The fear, the loving and being loved, the accounting for and the wish to had all become one.

Dream, where have you brought me? What a strange dream! Who would have thought to be here?

Beasts, angels, taking up room, the ways of duty and love: what next, dream, where now?

History

I have escaped in the dream; I was in danger, at peril, at immediate,
  furious, frightening risk,
but I deftly evaded the risk, eluded the danger, I conned peril to think
  I'd gone that way,
then I went this, then this way again, over the bridges of innocence, into
  the haven of sorrow.
I was so shrewd in my moment of risk, so cool: I was as guileful as though
  I were guilty,
sly, devious, cunning, though I'd done nothing in truth but be who I
  was where I was
when the dream conceived me as a threat I wasn't, possessed of a power
  I'd never had,
though I had found enough strength to flee and the guileful wherewithal
  to elude and be free.
I have escaped and survived, but as soon as I think it it starts again, I'm
  hounded again:
no innocence now, no unlikeliest way, only this frenzied combing of the
  countries of mind
where I always believed I'd find safety and solace but where now are
  confusion and fear
and a turmoil so total that all I have known or might know drags me
  with it towards chaos.
That, in this space I inhabit, something fearsome is happening, headlong,
  with an awful momentum,
is never in doubt, but that's all I can say—no way even to be sure if I'm
  victim or oppressor;
absurd after all this not to know if I'm subject or object, scapegoat,
  perpetrator, or prey.
The dream is of beings like me, assembled, surrounded, herded like
  creatures, driven, undone.
And beings like me, not more like me but like me, assemble and herd
  them, us; undo us.
No escape now, no survival: captured, subjugated, undone, we all move
  through dreams of negation.

Subject, object, dream doesn't care; accumulate or subtract, self as solace, self-blame.

Thou shalt, thou shalt not; thus do I, thus I do not: dream is indifferent, bemused, abstracted.

Formulation, abstraction; assembly, removal: the dream detached; exaltation, execration, denial.

The Gap

So often and with such cruel fascination I have dreamed the implacable
    void that contains dream.
The space there, the silence, the scrawl of trajectories tracked, traced,
    and let go;
the speck of matter in non-matter; sphere, swing, the puff of agglutinate
    loose-woven tissue;
the endless pull of absence on self, the sad molecule of the self in its
    chunk of duration;
the desolate grain, flake, fragment of mind that thinks when the mind
    thinks it's thinking.
So often, too, with equal absorption, I have dreamed the end of it all:
    mind, matter, void.
I'm appalled, but I do it again, I dream it again, it comes uncalled for
    but it comes, always,
rising perhaps out of the fearful demands consciousness makes for linkage,
    coherence, congruence,
connection to something beyond, even if dread: mystery exponentially
    functioned to dread.
Again, premonitions of silence, the swoop through a gulf that might be
    inherent in mind
as though mind bore in its matter its own end and the annulment of
    everything else.
Somehow I always return in the dream from the end, from the mean-
    ingless, the mesh of despair,
but what if I don't once, what if the corrections fail once and I can't
    recover the thread
that leads back from that night beyond night that absorbs night as night
    absorbs innocent day?
The whole of being untempered by self, the great selves beyond self all
    wholly wound out;
sense neutered, knowledge betrayed: what if this is the real end of dream,
    facing the darkness
and subjecting the self yet again to imperious laws of doubt and denial
    which are never repealed?

How much can I do this, how often rejuvenate and redeem with such
partial, imperfect belief?
So often, by something like faith, I'm brought back in the dream; but
this, too; so often this, too.

The Knot

Deciphering and encoding, to translate, fabricate, revise; the abstract star,
  the real star;
crossing over boundaries we'd never known were there until we found
  ourselves beyond them.
A fascination first: this was why the dream existed, so our definitions
  would be realized.
Then more than fascination as we grasped how dream could infiltrate
  the mundane with its radiance.
There'd be no mundane anymore: wholly given to the dream, our de-
  bilitating skepticisms overcome,
we'd act, or would be acted on—the difference, if there'd been one,
  would have been annulled—
with such purity of motive and such temperate desire that outcome would
  result from inspiration
with the same illumination that the notion of creation brings when it
  first comes upon us.
No question now of fabricating less ambiguous futures, no trying to recast
  recalcitrant beginnings.
It would be another empire of determination, in which all movement
  would be movement towards—
mergings, joinings—and in which existence would be generated from
  the qualities of our volition:
intention flowing outward into form and back into itself in intricate
  threadings and weavings,
intuitions shaped as logically as crystal forms in rock, a linkage at the
  incandescent core,
knots of purpose we would touch into as surely as we touch the rippling
  lattice of a song.
No working out of what we used to call identity; our consummations
  would consist of acts,
of participating in a consciousness that wouldn't need, because it grew
  from such pure need,
acknowledgment or subject: we'd be held in it, always knowing there
  were truths beyond it.

Cleansed even of our appetite for bliss, we'd only want to know the
  ground of our new wonder,
and we wouldn't be surprised to find that it survived where we'd known
  it had to all along,
in all for which we'd blamed ourselves, repented and corrected, and never
  for a moment understood.

The Fear

In my dream of unspecific anxiety, nothing is what it should be, nothing
    acts as it should;
everything shifts, shudders, won't hold still long enough for me to name
    or constrain it.
The fear comes with no premonition, no flicker in the daily surges and
    currents of dream.
Momentums, inertias, then logic distends, distorts, bends in convulsive
    postures of scorn.
All I hold dear rushes away in magnetic repulsion to me, ravaged as
    though by a storm,
but I know that I myself am the storm, I am the force that daunts,
    threatens, rages, repels.
I am like time, I gather the things of creation and drive them out from
    me towards an abyss.
All I call beauty is ravaged, transcendence hauled back in a gust to
    corporeal swarm.
I never believe that the part of me which is fear can raze all the rest with
    such fury,
even the flesh is depleted, forsaken; I'm no longer spirit or flesh but lost
    within both,
negated, forlorn, a thing the dream can capture and propel through itself
    any way it desires.
Nothing to hope for now but more concrete fears that at least might
    reveal their reason.
Nothing to dream but silence and forgetting; everything failing, even the
    wanting to be.

You

Such longing, such urging, such warmth towards, such force towards,
　　so much ardor and desire;
to touch, touch into, hold, hold against, to feel, feel against and long
　　towards again,
as though the longing, urge, and warmth were ends in themselves, the
　　increase of themselves,
the force towards, the ardor and desire, focused, increased, the incar-
　　nation of themselves.
All this in the body of dream, all in the substance of dream; allure,
　　attraction, and need,
the force so consumed and rapt in its need that dream might have evolved
　　it from itself,
except the ardor urges always towards the other, towards you, and without
　　you it decays,
becomes vestige, reflex, the defensive attempt to surmount instinctual
　　qualms and misgivings.
No qualms now, no misgivings; no hesitancy or qualifications in longing
　　towards you;
no frightened wish to evolve ideals to usurp qualm, fear or misgiving,
　　not any longer.
The longing towards you sure now, ungeneralized, certain, the urge now
　　towards you in yourself,
your own form of nearness, the surface of desire multiplied in the need
　　that urges from you,
your longing, your urging, the force and the warmth from you, the sure
　　ardor blazing in you.

To Listen

In the dream of death where I listen, the voices of the dream keep
    diminishing, fading away.
The dead are speaking, my dead are speaking, what they say seems urgent,
    to me, to themselves,
but as I try to capture more clearly what I heard just moments ago, the
    voices ebb and it's lost;
what's more, my impatience to know what was said seems to drive it
    further out of my ken.
In the dream of death where I listen, I keep thinking my dead have a
    message for me:
maybe they'll tell me at last why they must always die in the dream, live,
    die, die again.
I still can't hear what they say, though; I force my senses into the silence
    but nothing is there.
Sometimes I listen so hard I think what I'm waiting to hear must already
    have been spoken,
it's here, its echo surrounds me, I just have to learn to bring it more
    clearly within me
and I'll know at last what I never thought I would know about death and
    the dead and the speech
of affection the dead speak that stays on in the sentient space between
    living and after.
For the dead speak from affection, dream says, there's kindness in the
    voices of the dead.
I listen again, but I still hear only fragments of the elaborate discourse
    the dead speak;
when I try to capture its gist more is effaced, there are only faded words
    strewn on the page
of my soul that won't rest from its need to have what it thinks it can have
    from the dead.
Something is in me like greed now, I can't stop trying to tear the silence
    away from the voices,
I tear at the actual voices, though I know what the dead bring us is not
    to be held,

that the wanting to hold it is just what condemns dream to this pained,
      futile listening,
is what brings dream finally to its end, in silence, in want, in believing
      it's lost,
only for now, my dream thinks, at least let it be only for now, my forsaken
      dream thinks,
what the dead brought, what the dead found in their kind, blurred, weary
      voices to bring.

The Covenant

In my unlikeliest dream, my dead are with me again, companions again,
    in an ordinary way;
nothing of major moment to accomplish, no stains to cleanse, no oaths
    or debts to redeem:
my dead are serene, composed, as though they'd known all along how
    this would be.
Only I look aslant, only I brood and fret, marvel; only I have to know
    what this miracle is:
I'm awed, I want to embrace my newly found dead, to ask why they had
    to leave me so abruptly.
In truth, I think, I want pity from them, for my being bereft, for my
    grief and my pain.
But my dead will have none of my sorrow, of my asking how they came
    to be here again.
They anoint me with their mild regard and evidence only the need to
    continue, go on
in a dream that's almost like life in how only the plainest pastimes of
    love accumulate worth.
Cured of all but their presence, they seem only to want me to grasp their
    new way of being.
At first I feel nothing, then to my wonder and perhaps, too, the wonder
    of the dead,
I sense an absence in them, of will, of anything like will, as though will
    in the soul
had for the dead been all given over, transfigured, to humility, resig-
    nation, submission.
I know without knowing how that the dead can remember the movements
    of will, thought willing,
the gaze fixed at a distance that doesn't exist, the mind in its endless war
    with itself—
those old cravings—but the striving to will themselves from themselves
    is only a dream,
the dead know what death has brought is all they need now because all
    else was already possessed,

all else was a part of the heart as it lived, in what it had seen and what
it had suffered,
in the love it had hardly remarked coming upon it, so taken it was with
its work of volition.
I can hardly believe that so little has to be lost to find such good fortune
in death,
and then, as I dream again the suspensions of will I'm still only just able
to dream,
I suddenly know I've beheld death myself, and instead of the terror, the
flexions of fear,
the repulsion, recoil, impatience to finish, be done with the waiting once
and for all,
I feel the same surge of acceptance, patience, and joy I felt in my dead
rising in me:
I know that my dead have brought what I've restlessly waited all the life
of the dream for.
I wait in joy as they give themselves to the dream once again; waiting,
I'm with them again.

Light

Always in the dream I seemed conscious of myself having the dream even
 as I dreamed it.
Even now, the dream moving towards light, the field of light flowing
 gently towards me,
I watch myself dreaming, I watch myself dreaming and watching, I watch
 both watchers together.
It almost seems that this is what dream is about, to think what happens
 as it's happening.
Still, aren't there disturbing repercussions in being in such an active
 relation with dream?
What about nightmare, for instance; nightmare is always lurking there
 out at the edges,
it's part of dream's definition: how be so involved in the intimate workings
 of dream
without being an accomplice of nightmare, a portion of its cause or even
 its actual cause?
Doesn't what comes to me have to be my fault, and wouldn't the alter-
 native be more troubling still—
that I might *not* be the one engendering this havoc, that I'm only allowed
 to think so,
that the nightmare itself, hauling me through its vales of anguish, is the
 operative force?
What do I mean by nightmare itself, though? Wouldn't that imply a
 mind here besides mine?
But how else explain all the *care*, first to involve me, then to frighten
 me out of my wits?
Mustn't something with other agendas be shaping the dream; don't all
 the enticements and traps
suggest an intention more baleful than any I'd have for visiting such
 mayhem on myself?
And if this isn't the case, wouldn't the alternative be as bad; that each
 element of the dream
would contain its own entailment so that what came next would just do
 so for no special reason?

How frivolous dream would be, then: either way, though, so much
  subjugation, so little choice.
Either way, isn't the real nightmare my having so little power, *even over
  my own consciousness?*
Sometimes, when I arrive in dream here, when I arrive nearly over-
  whelmed with uncertainty here,
I feel a compulsion to renounce what so confounds me, to abdicate,
  surrender, but to what?
I don't even know if my despair might not be another deception the
  devious dream is proposing.
At last, sometimes, perhaps driven to this, perhaps falling upon it in
  exhaustion or resignation,
I try to recapture how I once dreamed, innocently, with no thought of
  being beside or beyond:
I imagine myself in that healing accord I still somehow believe must
  precede or succeed dream.
My vigilance never flags, though; I behold the infernal beholder, I behold
  the uncanny beheld,
this mind streaming through me, its turbulent stillness, its murmur,
  inexorable, beguiling.

5

Helen

More voice was in her cough tonight: its first harsh, stripping sound
 would weaken abruptly,
and he'd hear the voice again, not hers, unrecognizable, its notes from
 somewhere else,
someone saying something they didn't seem to want to say, in a tongue
 they hadn't mastered,
or a singer, diffident and hesitating, searching for a place to start an
 unfamiliar melody.

Its pitch was gentle, almost an interrogation, intimate, a plea, a moan,
 almost sexual,
but he could hear assertion, too, a straining from beneath, a forcing at
 the withheld consonant,
and he realized that she was holding back, trying with great effort not to
 cough again,
to change the spasm to a tone instead and so avert the pain that lurked
 out at the stress.

Then he heard her lose her almost-word, almost-song: it became a groan,
 the groan a gasp,
the gasp a sigh of desperation, then the cough rasped everything away,
 everything was cough now,
he could hear her shuddering, the voice that for a moment seemed the
 gentlest part of her,
choked down, effaced, abraded, taken back, as all of her was being taken
 from him now.

2

In the morning she was standing at the window; he lay where he was
 and quietly watched her.

A sound echoed in from somewhere, she turned to listen, and he was
    shocked at how she moved:
not *enough* moved, just her head, pivoting methodically, the mechanisms
    slowed nearly to a halt,
as though she was afraid to jar herself with the contracting tendons and
    skeletal leverings.

A flat, cool, dawn light washed in on her: how pale her skin was, how
    dull her tangled hair.
So much of her had burned away, and what was left seemed draped
    listlessly upon her frame.
It was her eye that shocked him most, though; he could only see her
    profile, and the eye in it,
without fire or luster, was strangely isolated from her face, and even from
    her character.

For the time he looked at her, the eye existed not as her eye, his wife's,
    his beloved's eye,
but as *an* eye, an object, so emphatic, so pronounced, it was separate
    both from what it saw
and from who saw with it: it could have been a creature's eye, a member
    of that larger class
which simply indicated sight and not that essence which her glance had
    always brought him.

It came to him that though she hadn't given any sign, she knew that he
    was watching her.
He was saddened that she'd tolerate his seeing her as she was now, weak,
    disheveled, haggard.
He felt that they were both involved, him watching, her letting him, in
    a depressing indiscretion:
she'd always, after all their time together, only offered him the images
    she thought he wanted.

She'd known how much he needed beauty, how much presumed it as
    the elemental of desire.
The loveliness that illuminated her had been an engrossing narrative his
    spirit fed on;

94

he entered it and flowed out again renewed for having touched within
   and been a part of it.
In his meditations on her, he'd become more complicated, fuller, more
   essential to himself.

It was to her beauty he'd made love at first, she was there within its
   captivating light,
but was almost secondary, as though she was just the instance of some
   overwhelming generality.
She herself was shy before it; she, too, as unassumingly as possible was
   testing this abstraction
which had taken both of them into its sphere, rendering both subservient
   to its serene enormity.

As their experience grew franker, and as she learned to move more
   confidently towards her core,
became more overtly active in elaborating needs and urges, her beauty
   still came first.
In his memory, it seemed to him that they'd unsheathed her from the
   hazes of their awe,
as though her unfamiliar, fiery, famished nakedness had been disclosed
   as much to her as him.

She'd been grateful to him, and that gratitude became in turn another
   fact of his desire.
Her beauty had acknowledged him, allowed him in its secret precincts,
   let him be its celebrant,
an implement of its luxurious materiality, and though he remained as-
   tonished by it always,
he fulfilled the tasks it demanded of him, his devotions reinvigorated and
   renewed.

3

In the deepest sense, though, he'd never understood what her beauty was
   or really meant.

If you only casually beheld her, there were no fanfares, you were taken
by no immolating ecstasies.
It amused him sometimes seeing other men at first not really understand-
ing what they saw;
no one dared to say it, but he could feel them holding back their dis-
appointment or disbelief.

Was this Helen, mythic Helen, this female, fleshed like any other, im-
perfect and approachable?
He could understand: he himself, when he'd first seen her, hadn't really;
he'd even thought,
before he'd registered her spirit and intelligence, before her laughter's
melodies had startled him—
if only one could alter such and such, improve on this or that: he hardly
could believe it now.

But so often he'd watched others hear her speak, or laugh, look at her
again, and fall in love,
as puzzled as he'd been at the time they'd wasted while their raptures of
enchantment took.
Those who hadn't ever known her sometimes spoke of her as though she
were his thing, his toy,
but that implied something static in her beauty, and she was surely just
the opposite of that.

If there was little he'd been able to explain of what so wonderfully ab-
sorbed him in her,
he knew it was a movement and a process, that he was taken towards
and through her beauty,
touched by it but even more participating in its multiplicities, the rev-
elations of its grace.
He felt himself becoming real in her, tangible, as though before he'd
only half existed.

Sometimes he would even feel it wasn't really him being brought to such
unlikely fruition.
Absurd that anyone so coarse and ordinary should be in touch with such
essential mystery:

something else, beyond him, something he would never understand,
   used him for its affirmations.
What his reflections came to was something like humility, then a gratitude
   of his own.

4

The next night her cough was worse, with a harsher texture, the spasms
   came more rapidly,
and they'd end with a deep, complicated emptying, like the whining
   flattening of a bagpipe.
The whole event seemed to need more labor: each cough sounded more
   futile than the last,
as though the effort she'd made and the time lost making it had added
   to the burden of illness.

Should he go to her? He felt she'd moved away from him, turning more
   intently towards herself.
Her sickness absorbed her like a childbirth; she seemed almost like some-
   one he didn't know.
There'd been so many Helens, the first timid girl, then the sensual Helen
   of their years together,
then the last, whose grace had been more intricate and difficult to know
   and to exult in.

How childishly frightened he'd always been by beauty's absence, by its
   destruction or perversity.
For so long he let himself be tormented by what he knew would have to
   happen to her.
He'd seen the old women as their thighs and buttocks bloated, then
   withered and went slack,
as their dugs dried, skin dried, legs were sausaged with the veins that rose
   like kelp.

He'd tried to overcome himself, to feel compassion towards them, but,
   perhaps because of her,

he'd felt only a shameful irritation, as though they were colluding in
    their loss.
Whether they accepted what befell them, even, he would think, gladly
    acquiescing to it,
or fought it, with all their sad and valiant unguents, dyes, and ointments,
    was equally degrading.

His own body had long ago become a ruin, but beauty had never been
    a part of what he was.
What would happen to his lust, and to his love, when time came to
    savage and despoil her?
He already felt his will deserting him; for a long time, though, nothing
    touched or dulled her:
perhaps she really was immortal, maybe his devotion kept her from the
    steely rakings of duration.

Then, one day, something at her jowls; one day her hips; one day the
    flesh at her elbows . . .
One day, one day, one day he looked at her and knew that what he'd
    feared so was upon them.
He couldn't understand how all his worst imaginings had come to pass
    without his noticing.
Had he all this while been blind, or had he not wanted to acknowledge
    what he'd dreaded?

He'd been gazing at her then; in her wise way, she'd looked back at him,
    and touched him,
and he knew she'd long known what was going on in him: another
    admiration took him,
then another fire, and that simply, he felt himself closer to her: there'd
    been no trial,
nothing had been lost, of lust, of love, and something he'd never dreamed
    would be was gained.

5

With her in the darkness now, not even touching her, he sensed her
    fever's suffocating dryness.

He couldn't, however much he wanted to, not let himself believe she
    was to be no more.
And there was nothing he could do for her even if she'd let him; he tried
    to calm himself.
Her cough was hollow, soft, almost forgiving, ebbing slowly through the
    volumes of her thorax.

He could almost hear that world as though from in her flesh: the current
    of her breath,
then her breastbone, ribs, and spine, taking on the cough's vibrations,
    giving back their own.
Then he knew precisely how she was within herself as well, he was with
    her as he'd never been:
he'd unmoored in her, cast himself into the night of her, and perceived
    her life with her.

All she'd lived through, all she'd been and done, he could feel accu-
    mulated in this instant.
The impressions and sensations, feelings, dreams, and memories were
    tearing loose in her,
had disconnected from each other and randomly begun to float, collide,
    collapse, entangle;
they were boiling in a matrix of sheer chance, suspended in a purely
    mental universe of possibility.

He knew that what she was now to herself, what she remembered, might
    not in truth have ever been.
Who, then, was she now, who was the person she had been, if all she
    was, all he still so adored,
was muddled, addled, mangled: what of her could be repository now,
    the place where she existed?
When everything was shorn from her, what within this flux of fragments
    still stayed her?

He knew then what he had to do: he was so much of her now and she
    of him that she was his,
her consciousness and memory both his, he would will her into him,
    keep her from her dissolution.
All the wreckage of her fading life, its shattered hours taken in this fearful
    flood,

its moments unrecoverable leaves twirling in a gust across a waste of loss,
    he drew into himself,

and held her, kept her, all the person she had been was there within his
    sorrow and his longing:
it didn't matter what delirium had captured her, what of her was being
    lacerated, rent,
his pain had taken on a power, his need for her became a force that he
    could focus on her;
there was something in him like triumph as he shielded her within the
    absolute of his affection.

Then he couldn't hold it, couldn't keep it, it was all illusion, a confection
    of his sorrow:
there wasn't room within the lenses of his mortal being to contain what
    she had been,
to do justice to a single actual instant of her life and soul, a single moment
    of her mind,
and he released her then, let go of this diminished apparition he'd created
    from his fear.

But still, he gave himself to her, without moving moved to her: she was
    still his place of peace.
He listened for her breath: was she still here with him, did he have her
    that way, too?
He heard only the flow of the silent darkness, but he knew now that in
    it they'd become it,
their shells of flesh and form, the old delusion of their separateness and
    incompletion, gone.

When one last time he tried to bring her image back, she was as vivid
    as he'd ever seen her.
What they were together, everything they'd lived, all that seemed so
    fragile, bound in time,
had come together in him, in both of them: she had entered death, he
    was with her in it.
Death was theirs, she'd become herself again; her final, searing loveliness
    had been revealed.